Contents

Chapter	Title	Page
Foward		2
1	I Made This Job Look Easy	4
2	Strike Two	22
3	Chameleon-Like Bitches	24
4	Gaslight	28
5	Ted Messed With The Wrong Bitch	34
6	Jordan Is Not Acting Like A Supervisor	35
7	Bitch Ass Jordan	38
8	A Video Is Worth A Million Words	59
9	Don't I Give You Compliments	61
10	The Harsh Reality	62
11	What The Fuck	90
12	Take Notes	95
13	Fuck You Adriana	97

Thanks to everyone

https://donttakenoshitdocument.com/

Forward
Power Grubbing Bitches

I'll admit, I'm a power-grubbing bitch like all of the co-workers, supervisors, and managers I'd crossed paths with during my employment within a public school's Facilities Department. Oh, and by the way, I'll also admit my mother was a fucking lunatic, and she taught me everything she knew.

Hello, my name is Alexandra King, formerly employed 'Custodian Helper' for the Public School district in my state. The 'Good Ole Boys' culture that existed inside the Facilities department gave life to its wicked master-slave mentality. I'd swear it was like working for the Trump administration. Except I'd worked with a bunch of insecure assholes masquerading as co-workers, supervisors, and managers, rather than racist and inept white con men masquerading as politicians.

Every supervisor and manager I'd encountered at this job had an insatiable appetite for sabotaging their employees. Which led me to believe that backstabbing was a prerequisite for being promoted. Those toxic employees loved creating disharmony in the workplace.

This book was my reward for doing what was right at the time, annihilating the, 'Good Ole Boys' master-slave mentality. Hope you enjoy my exposé of a Public School's dirty little secrets.

Chapter One
I Made This Job Look Easy

I was offered and accepted a part-time custodian job in October 2016. My hours were from 5 pm to 9 pm. However, this was not my first cleaning job, and if you know me, you know not to fuck with me when cleanliness is my job. If you are easily offended by me, that's not my problem. Don't get it twisted, being a custodian was a physical job. At my age, I had my doubts about my physical fitness and if I could last more than a week.

I kid you not; I also had doubts about this job because I'd instinctively knew my responsibilities were intended for a full-time employee. Remember, I was a part-time employee. That underhanded tactic was just the tip of the iceberg to all the corruption that existed in the workplace. Hard working employees didn't have a chance of surviving. Leaving the term,'Short Staffed,' a permanent status inside the custodian department. One of the negative consequences of being 'Short Staffed,' was that it cultivated and attracted Slackers. Some of my co-workers believed their responsibilities as a Custodian, or as a Supervisor or Manager was leaving the property for hours, or smoking weed and hiding out in a dark room, or endlessly socializing, or being on the computer in the breakroom or office, or being on an extended lunch break, or talking on their cell phones. It was obvious that time thief was held in high esteem. There was honor among thieves.

However, I had fun destroying those Slacker's mistaken belief that I would become their labor slave. How'd you like me now?

As challenging as it was doing a full-time job on part-time hours, the pay was another clever way of sabotaging employees. Because to earn more money, you had to become a slithering snake in the grass for your supervisor and manager. That meant sabotaging hard working employees. Let me put it to you this way, the 'Good Ole Boys' master-slave mentality was Kryptonite for hard working employees. But, I'd thrived in this habitat because the hunter, i.e. Slackers became my prey.

It was inevitable that a person like me who saw straight through the bullshit in this toxic environment would give those sniveling ass bitches, i.e., Slackers my middle finger. A fuck I didn't give to their lazy, trifling asses.

I made my job look easy, not because I have some special powers, but because I was focused, disciplined, and more importantly, I was dependable. My initial intentions were to work until I'd reached the age of sixty-two then retire on Social Security. A boring retirement plan that went off the rails into a ditch. Oh, trust me, this book was a birds nest on the ground.

During the week-long Housekeeping class that was mandatory for new employees, our instructor referred to our assignments as a 'Run.' He painted this picture that Custodians had a combination of classrooms and restrooms to clean every day. That we'd do the same cleaning each day and become so efficient to the degree that we'd glide through our, 'Run.' That we'd be able to clean areas like windows, ceiling exhausts vents, and other areas not included in our initial, 'Run.' Well, he was wrong.

The first school that I was assigned to work was a Middle/High School. It served students from grades 6-12. To my surprise, I was responsible for cleaning classrooms only, no restrooms. I was thrilled. However, my tenure at that first school lasted five months. After that, I'd transferred to another school into a full-time custodian position. But before I tell you about that second school's sabotaging, this first school's sabotaging was an omen. My 'Run' consisted of classrooms on the first and second floors. There were two types of classrooms, carpeted or tiled. The standard time allotted for vacuuming a carpeted classroom was ten minutes, while the standard time allotted for cleaning a tile classroom was twenty minutes.

This particular school also had an 'A,' 'B' schedule. Meaning I'd clean all the assigned classrooms on the first floor on one day and the next day clean all the assigned classrooms on the second floors. I'd referred to this, 'A' 'B' schedule as **'Fucked Up.'** Seriously, because everyday students would trash each classroom until it looked like an episode of Hoarders. This schedule to clean each classroom every other day proved untenable even for me, because of the time allotted to clean this mess. Ten minutes to vacuum a carpeted room with debris from corner to corner, was a fucking fantasy. It took approximately five minutes per room to pick up the trash off the floor that was too big or too heavy to vacuum up. Then throw it away in the trash bin. Did I mention that the vacuums we used were backpack vacuums? Yes, some asshole thought it was a good idea to purchase these backpack style vacuums. What a fucking waste of money is all I can say.

The tile rooms were worse than the carpeted rooms. Students would trash the floors, sinks, and counters. These rooms were huge with up to ten sinks. It took more than the allotted time of twenty minutes to clean up the fucking mess left in those rooms. Those rooms also had hands free paper towel and soap dispensers that often required refilling. Like the carpeted classrooms, these rooms got cleaned every other day, so the amount of mess doubled by the time I'd entered to clean it.

Although I'd cleverly created a more sustainable strategy, one I could live with, that was unique to me. What I did was divided my four hours into two hours of vacuuming classrooms and two hours for cleaning tile classrooms. One of the benefits of my strategy, it made me look like superwoman because it worked. So, in a way, I do understand why that sorry ass Facilities Manager named Bob tried to sabotage me. Before I get to that, check this out, in some of the larger tiled classrooms if the 50 plus chairs and stools were still on the floor, I had to perform the task of placing them up on the tables and counters in order to sweep and mop the floor. Truthfully, it took a lot of determination to remain on that job, because in the back of my mind, I'd believed then as I do today, our children deserved clean schools.

However, it had occurred to me, on more than one occasion that maybe I was the reason why those idiots masquerading as managers, believed I was superhuman. The consistency of those sniveling bitches aka Facilities Managers to assigned more work to me became their undoing.

But like I'd mentioned, I had my cross to bear. There were times early on at that first job when I had my doubts. Because of the physical labor involved. I'm a Grandma, so without revealing my age... I'll just say that much. But, that job was whipping me into shape, so it turned out for the best.

It was obvious to me that the standard of cleanliness was so low at this first school because those idiots in the custodian department were so insecure and quite frankly lazy ass bitches. They couldn't help but throw shade at me with their annoying *"We don't have time for that,"* whenever they saw me cleaning. Referring to my cleaning as, 'Deep Cleaning.' I personally believed, which was the reason why I wasn't mad at them, that those men had inherited their misogynistic attitudes. The work environment was a real life, 'Good Ole Boys Club.'

I'd immediately realized I was the only female on the night shift. Also, that my cleaning habits probably scared the fuck out of my male co-workers. A war was brewing, males vs. female in the battle of con vs. wits.

First off, I was horrified by the 'A' 'B' schedule. It meant that every night only half the classrooms assigned to me were cleaned. It also meant students had two days to trash a room before I'd clean it. As crazy as that was, we already operated on a skeleton crew, so if a co-worker called in, or abruptly quit, the shit hit the fan. Instead of cleaning any of my assigned classrooms, the focus was emptying trash throughout the school and cleaning restrooms. Not by myself, but with the few co-workers who'd managed to show up at work.

The hierarchy in this Good Ole Boys Club began with the Area Manager. His name was Mateo Lopez. He was, in my opinion, the most inept and superficial Manager I'd met since Holly. Holly was the manager for the retail store where I'd worked before this custodian job. Second, the Facilities Manager at this Middle/High school was named Jose Rodriguez. My first conversation with Jose was over the phone, and I swear Jose's voice confused the hell out of me. He sounded like Michael McDonald, i.e. 'What a fool believes,' while his last name was of Hispanic heritage. After meeting him, it was obvious he was born Hispanic but lived in or impersonated a black culture. No sooner after our initial meeting, Jose abruptly quit, I mean no notice at all. What did came to light was Jose's extracurricular activities at work. Or abruptly stated, Jose's scandalous behavior caught up with him. After Jose's disappearing act, that meant that the Night Supervisor, a young black man named Tyrell became the interim Facilities Manager. Tyrell then moved to the day shift. That left Bryan, an even younger black man in charge of the night crew. For the next two months, we operated from a disadvantage, i.e., short staffed. Which is a segway for me to introduce the slacker extraordinaire and co-worker named, Willis. Willis's ego was enormous, wider than the Atlantic ocean. Seriously, he acted like he was in charge of the night crew. Willis was an older black man. He strutted around the school, referred to everyone as, 'Shorty,' and bragged about having a baby momma. I must tell you that at first, I wasn't privy to all the torrid details of this immaculate conception, but when I was, it made me laugh out loud. Apparently, Willis was going to be a dad for the second time, but this second baby momma was a professional Stripper. It seemed Willis and Bryan loved going to strip clubs so you can imagine how high Willis believed his stock was worth at our workplace. Willis and I were the same age, so you can only imagine my thoughts when he bragged about having a baby momma. And this was before I knew she was a professional Stripper. Don't get your panties in a bunch because I'm not judging the profession known as, 'Dancing for money.' I have mad respect for Strippers as much as I have for myself. C'mon, in the end, we're all women, capable of being the good, the bad, and the ugly. Ima say this, did she know that Willis didn't own a car? And after hearing a little about his home life, did she know that he lived with another woman? So, I was just curious about this Stripper's judgment. Willis did have one of the best strategies going for him. He'd befriended Tyrell and Bryan. They were the three Amigos until a new Facilities Manager named Bob arrived in January of the new year. However, by February of that same year the shit hit the fan, Aretha (my alter ego) made her debut, and by April I'd transferred to another school.

To say that Willis was annoying would have been an understatement. This fool didn't have two dimes to rub together, yet it didn't stop him from saying the most inappropriate things to Tyrell. Unbeknownst to me, Willis was a part-time Custodian, yet he was working full-time hours. After the new Facilities Manager named Bob arrived at this school, he discovered one of Jose's dirty little secrets. Jose had approved Willis's full-time status without going through the proper channels. So immediately Willis was stripped of his full-time hours.

Bob, the new Facilities Manager, was a burly white man, he looked more like a lumberjack. After he was officially on board, he showed up one night to introduce himself to the night crew. We were all gathered inside a room resembling an executive boardroom and seated at a large oval table in very comfortable leather chairs. Bob introduced himself to everyone except Tyrell. Tyrell had a scheduled day off. Towards the end of this meet-n-greet farce, I'd asked Bob why this school had an 'A' 'B' schedule. His response was straight outta the Twilight Zone. Some bullshit about once upon a time when the custodial staff was larger. They'd cleaned every classroom, but completed their 'Runs' way ahead of time and would be on

the clock sitting around with nothing to do. So according to Bob, this school was wasting money paying employees to sit around. Therefore the decision was made to implement an 'A' 'B' schedule and lay off the 'excess' Custodians.
Yeah, if that sounds crazy to you, imagine how I'd felt.

When I saw Tyrell the next day, I couldn't wait to get the truth out of him about this, 'A' 'B' schedule. Curiously I said to Tyrell, *'Tyrell, what's up with Bob, he told me...blah, blah, blah.* Tyrell's facial expression said it all. Of course, you know what Tyrell said. He said that the only reason this school implemented an 'A' 'B' cleaning schedule was that it couldn't keep a full staff. Booyah and Amen were the words going through my mind. I knew it; Bob was just blowing smoke up my ass.

Also in January 2017, this school's Facilities Department had inherited a brand new ECE (Early Childhood Education) school located a few blocks away. It was Bob's responsibility to hire a full-time custodian to clean the classrooms/restrooms/offices and cafeteria. I'm not sure why, but within a month, the newly hired custodian for this ECE school went from fulltime to part-time. Bob's decision to send

Willis to work part-time at the ECE school was in my opinion, 'Fucked up.' At this time, Willis and I were the only part-time employees. Unbeknownst to me at this time, but it came to light during the last week before I'd left this school, that Willis was a predator. It seemed that several female employees at the Middle/High school had complained about Willis's behavior towards them. This was before Willis was sent over to the ECE school. Tyrell was fully aware of Willis's propensity to talk inappropriately to women but apparently didn't inform Bob. Or he had informed Bob and Bob didn't give a fuck and sent Willis to work at the ECE school knowing that the entire staff was female. Then, the next thing I knew, Bob decided that I should vacuum all the carpeted classrooms on one floor, while Tyrell cleaned all the tile classrooms at the Middle/High school. Instead of being upfront with me with this reckless, harmful, and terrible idea, I was misled every day for an entire week. First, Tyrell told me that Willis was scheduled to work at the ECE school for one week, but didn't tell me that I'd be vacuuming rooms every day for my entire four-hour shift. No, that slick bitch waited until after I'd arrive at work each day, then told me to vacuum rooms for my entire shift. That charade went on for one week because, by Friday, my back was extremely sore because of the vacuum from hell, i.e., a backpack vacuum.

That and how I was led to believe by Tyrell that Willis would be returning from the ECE school after one week. Well, that didn't happen, and on the following Monday Tyrell had the same fucked up task for me to do. Well, that's when my other persona came out. Unfortunately for Tyrell, he got to meet my lunatic mother, 'Aretha.' Aretha transitioned in 2002, but made her debut through me on that Monday evening in February 2017. Of all places to make her debut, my mother's persona chose a public school building. I told you, she was a lunatic.

Some of you may know what I'm talking about, because unbeknownst to me before that moment, I hadn't realized that I'd inherited my mother's lunatic behavior to 'fuss' at someone endlessly. Aretha spoke through me and told Tyrell in so many words, *'Listen, you sniveling little bitch, ya better back the fuck off.'* Because what came out of my mouth was pure Aretha. Suffice it to say, Aretha scared the bejesus out of Tyrell. She let him know that his plans to coerce me into a labor slave ended that evening.

After arriving to work, Tyrell told me, *"Just do the same thing you did last week, vacuuming the classrooms."* I didn't hesitate and told Tyrell, *"I can't do it...my back is sore, and I don't appreciate working my ass off, while Willis is over at the other school on vacation."* Tyrell admitted that Willis wasn't working and that Bob was going to have a talk with him [Willis] about his lack of work. That omission fueled my rage. Then Tyrell asked me, *"Well, what are you going to do?"* I told him I would vacuum the classrooms originally assigned to me, and since Willis wasn't working over at the ECE school, he should come back to this school and vacuum the classrooms assigned to him. I'd also told Tyrell that because my back was sore, I'd place that hellish vacuum on the floor while vacuuming and yes, it would take a longer time to complete that task. Tyrell told me he had to call Bob and scurried away. I can only imagine how that conversation went. Tyrell probably said to Bob, *'Bob, that bitch is crazy, she's talkin' shit about workin' her ass off, while Willis is on vacation.'* I can almost hear Bob's reply, *'Tell that bitch to vacuum her rooms only, and I'll call you back to let you know what else she can do.'* The next thing I knew, Tyrell reported to me that after I'd vacuumed my assigned classrooms that Bob wanted me to remove gum from the classroom carpets. Anyone in the cleaning business knows what I'm talking about when I say, that task was punishment. Removing gum from any carpet is futile. This public school district could replace the carpets in every classroom, every year, and still have millions of dollars to overpay inept Facility Managers. However, during my break, two hours later, I went face to face with Tyrell or should I said, 'Aretha' went face to face with Tyrell. All Tyrell could say to me was that I was being insubordinate. I'd inquired why I wasn't chosen to work at the ECE school. Tyrell responded that Mateo went by seniority. At that time I'd foolishly believed him. It was true that Willis and I were the only part-time employees and Willis had seniority, so it made sense. But during this time Bob hired another part-time employee, a young Hispanic female. She worked two days and disappeared, leaving me to believe she had quit. Inadvertently, I'd found out she was transferred over to the ECE school because the staff had complained about Willis's behavior. So much for seniority. That was the straw that broke the camel's back, and by April of 2017, I'd transferred to another school.

Tyrell and I didn't talk for over a week after Aretha's **'Bitch I didn't raise no labor slave,'** sermon. Now imagine Tyrell's and Bob's surprise when they found out approximately two months later that I'd kept my promise to leave this, 'Good Ole Boys Club.' I'd applied for a transfer, and Mateo approved it.

What was waiting for me at the next school was a doozy of a story.

Chapter Two
Strike Two

Ted was the Facilities Manager at the next school. This school also served grades 6-12. Ted was a middle-aged, misogynistic white man, intent on fulfilling his GOD complex, by any means necessary. That led me to believe that Ted was nothing more than a sniveling bitch-ass coward.

Next up was a Custodian Helper named Jordan. He was young, black, and a wanna be gangsta. Jordan played Ted like a violin, but underneath his gangsta persona, Jordan was an insecure little momma's boy. Jordan did whatever he wanted to do while at work, and time thief was on the top of his list.

A younger woman named Rachel worked as a part-time custodian, and she completed our staff. She was an extremely smart and courageous woman. I can't say anything bad about Rachel. She eventually left a week before I'd left this school, because Ted tried over and over again to bully her, but she gave Ted the middle finger.

However, a younger guy named Alejandro joined our team two months after my start date at this school, and it wasn't a secret that he was one of Mateo's apprentices. Alejandro was young, Hispanic, with a lucrative future within this public school. Alejandro threw me under the bus so fast that even I was impressed.

Chapter Three
Chameleon-Like Bitches

"You do pay attention to the small details," Ted said to me while sizing me up like a labor slave on my second day of employment with this school. Come to think of it, that's why he immediately changed my hours. I went from a shift that began at 2 pm and ended at 10:30 pm, to the shift from noon to 8:30 pm. What soon came to light was that Ted suffered from a GOD complex. After five months of working with this idiot, his GOD complex had left the building.

Jordan was the interim night supervisor when I'd arrived at this second school. Ted had no one else to seduce into that position after the rightful Night Supervisor went out on FMLA. Jordan's normal shift was from 5:30 am until 2 pm. But after the Night Supervisor named John went on FMLA, Mateo obviously had Ted seduce Jordan into becoming the interim Night Supervisor. I'd join this staff on April 3, 2017, but by the end of May 2017, Jordan was unceremoniously removed from the Night Supervisor position and went back to his normal shift. Rachel and I had exposed Jordan's corrupt behavior, and

Mateo had no choice but to remove Jordan from the Night Supervisor position. Jordan had been a very, very bad boy, until he met, 'Aretha.'

Like I'd mentioned before, within my first week at this school, Ted changed my schedule to accommodate Jordan's absence from the day shift. That and the fact that Ted was a sniveling and lazy bitch ass coward. In Ted's world, intimidation, bullying, and misogyny ruled. However, Ted was no match for, 'Aretha.' After 'Aretha' got through wiping the floor with Ted, he knew he had been playing checkers, while 'she' was playing chess.

So, after my hours changed, the cafeteria became part of my 'Run' and get this I had an 'A' 'B' 'C' schedule. That meant cleaning the classrooms every third day. That was also FUCKED UP! By the time I went into each classroom to clean, it was deplorable. Listen, parents, you should check out your kid's classrooms. If they aren't clean every night, you should sue the school to make sure your children aren't going to school and sitting in trashy, smelly classrooms.

After I told Jordan that my hours were changed, you should have seen Jordan whined like a baby. Seriously, Jordan acted like a jealous bitch. He had the audacity to tell me, "*Ted doesn't need you to come in early, he can do that, he doesn't need you coming in at twelve ... You should've told him no.*" Seriously, Jordan sounded like a jealous twelve-year-old bitch. Like Ted had chosen me over him. He seriously demanded that I tell Ted no. I'd said to myself, '*Fuck you Jordan.*'

Inevitable I was burdened with some of Jordan's responsibilities because his lazy ass left the property every day for hours. His punk ass never answered the radio and was never around to help me or anyone else. As scandalous as that was, I knew that Jordan received a siphon for being the Night Supervisor. So it was safe to say, Jordan was a thieving asshole.

On my first day, I wasn't on the clock for five minutes when Jordan began berating Ted. Jordan told me how lazy Ted was, how nobody like him, how he got demoted from another school, and other vile and vicious gossip. Truthfully, Jordan spent a great deal of time berating Ted to me and to anyone who would listen. Like I'd mentioned, my shift started at noon,

Jordan's shift started every day at 2 pm, and it was at 2 pm that we were scheduled to clean the cafeteria. After stacking all the chairs, folding all the lunch tables, and moving them against the walls, we would sweep and mop the floor. After that task, Jordan would disappear. It was obvious to Rachel and me that Jordan left the property only to return hours later to lock up.

Conversations between Jordan and I came to an abrupt halt within one week. Jordan was also a religious freak. He tried to apotheosize his co-workers while at work with some bizarre shit about Blacks, Hispanics, and Native Americans all going to heaven while White people were destined to go to hell. Seriously, he would download bible scriptures on his cell phone that he claimed White people didn't want us to know. After one day of Jordan's apotheosizing, I'd kept my distance from his crazy ass. We barely spoke to one another, and that was fine by me. One thing I did notice was that Jordan's work phone was permanently stuck to his ear while we cleaned the cafeteria. It was obvious that his conversations were personal, not professional.

Chapter Four
Gaslight

Ted began a campaign to, 'Gaslight' my ass early on because he believed I was his new labor slave. Ted thought he could coerce me into cleaning the entryways. He tried to use the Q & A reviews to gaslight my ass. He'd wrote shit like I wasn't a team player or that I was too slow. In reality, a fuck I gave to Ted's weak ass opinions of me. I'd told his sniveling bitch ass early on that I didn't have time to clean those entryways and I was telling the truth. How fucked up in the head was Ted? Well, let me count the ways. First, Jordan played Ted like a violin. Second, Ted looked at me as a labor slave. Third Ted demanded I respect his stupid ass. Yes, that wussy went there, he'd threatened to fire me unless I respected him.

On May 11, 2017, Rachel had called Ted at approximately 2 pm and reported that she wasn't coming to work. Ted immediately decided to alter my schedule to accommodate Rachel's absence. Ted entered the cafeteria while Jordan was standing right next to me and proceeded to tell us that Rachel had called in sick and that he wanted me to trash Rachel's area as well as clean her hallway restrooms. Also, he instructed me to trash my area and do my hallway restrooms and clean the entryways. Before Ted could get out of hearing range, Jordan went into a pretend rage. He expressed to me how aghast he was that Ted had given me too much work. C'mon, who was he fooling? Not me, because I knew Jordan didn't give a fuck about me, yet there he was, doing his best impersonation of a black-faced Al Jolson. *"Oh, Alexandra, Ted gave you too much work...he wants you to trash Rachel's area, do her restrooms, and trash your floor and do your restrooms and entryways...that too much work...c'mon let's go talk to him...you have to tell him that's too much work...c'mon...I'll go with you...we betta hurry because he'll be leaving..."* Did Jordan seriously think I'd fall for his fake apathy? If Jordan cared so much, why didn't he say something to Ted while he was standing in front of us? The next thing I knew, 'Aretha' rose up inside me and took Jordan down to the woodshed. I'd put my hand on my hip, my other arm bent at my elbow, my forefinger pointed to Jordan's face and my head slightly tilted as if I was saying, "**Bitch are you seriously.'** Then I'd proceeded to explain to Jordan *"Look, the only reason why Ted gives me more work because you're not here, you're gone, you leave, and Ted knows you leave."*

Well, things went from bad to worse for Jordan, because I didn't let up. I told him exactly what he didn't want to hear. That his sorry ass wasn't fooling me, and that I knew he was leaving the property, and that Ted knew all about it. I'd also told that sorry bitch Jordan that I'd already told Ted I didn't have time to clean those entryways and that Ted doesn't listen to me. So, no, I wasn't interested in talking to Ted. Well, all Jordan could say in his defense was, *"That may be."* But you know what, Jordan quickly figured out he wasn't going to play me like a violin, and he went running out the cafeteria into Ted's arms. Because the next thing I knew, Jordan came back and arrogantly announced that I did have time to clean those entryways because Ted showed him the 'Core Standards.' Again I gave him my '**Bitch are you serious**' look and continued working. Then approximately an hour later, Jordan approached me with some more bullshit. He said, *"I was just talkin' to Ted, and he said whatever you don't finish, just leave him a note."* Again, I gave Jordan my '**Bitch are you serious**' look and said, *"Ted has eyes...when he comes to work tomorrow, he can see what was done, and what wasn't done."* Then I turned and walked away from that sniveling bitch-ass coward.

Trust me I had no idea how deplorable Rachel's area was because she worked on the second floor. Each classroom was filthy. I couldn't believe what I saw, classroom after classroom trashed, filthy, and disgusting. Oh, the restrooms were worse. The entire floor was a complete nightmare. The only thing I regret was that I didn't take one picture that night. Weeks later, after Rachel approached me and asked me to look at one of the restrooms on the second floor, was the only picture I'd recorded. It's the picture I'd used for the cover of this book. In essence, it represents how every classroom and every restroom looked like on the second floor.

Of course, when I'd told Ted the next day after Rachel had called in and I was instructed to clean her area, how deplorable those classrooms and restrooms looked, he tried to blame Rachel. I wasn't falling for Ted's blame game. I knew Ted was the only reason why the second floor looked so disgusting because Ted was as inept as he was lazy.

Unbeknownst to me, Rachel had emailed Ted complaining about Jordan's toxic behavior on the day she'd was absent from work. The next day Friday, May 12, 2017, Ted called me into his office and proceeded to tell me that Rachel and I had similar complaints about Jordan. It was obvious that Jordan told Ted what I'd said about him leaving the property. Like a snake in the grass, Ted insinuated that Rachel and I were in cahoots and planned this 'assault' on Jordan. At this point, I didn't expect anything less from Ted. Suffice it to say; I wasn't surprised that Ted started defending Jordan. That didn't stop me from telling Ted about some of Jordan's other toxic behavior like constantly being on his cell phone. Ted knew what Rachel and I told him about Jordan was closer to the truth, than fiction, because he told me he would talk with Jordan.

The following week, I'd noticed that Jordan wasn't on his cell phone and that it was obvious that Ted had spoken to him. Well, that didn't last long, because by Friday, May 19, 2017, Jordan entered the cafeteria and the following events happened that day.

From: King, Alexandra
Sent: Friday, May 19, 2017 8:29 PM
To: Rogers, Ted
Cc: Lopez_Mateo@xxxx.xxx
Subject: Offensive Language

Today at approximately 2:30pm, Jordan Thomas, Joey (floater) and myself were in the cafeteria cleaning. Jordan was on the phone and within minutes his voice was raised and he said, "That bitch needs to worry about what she's doing around here and stop worrying about what I'm doing around here." To which Joey laughed.

That same day, approximately 6:45pm, Jordan told me I had to clean the restrooms on the 2nd floor, per Ted, because Rachel had called in. Truth be told, I don't trust Jordan to tell me the truth. If he's comfortable publicly demeaning someone while at work, cause I'd believed he was talking about me. I could be wrong, but it's how I'd felt. For all I know, Ted told Jordan to clean those restrooms.

Chapter Five
Ted Messed With The Wrong Bitch

If a picture is worth a thousand words, then a video is worth a million words. It was more than obvious to me that Ted didn't give a fuck about cleaning up this school. It also was no secret that Jordan flaunted his power over Ted, which made it extremely difficult for me to respect Ted. But Ted pretended that he was the manager of the decade. In reality, Ted was Jordan's ass wipe.

Just want to say this before I go on with my story, I'd also worked in the Retail Industry. Although the company I'd worked for promotes, 'Magic' believe me there was no magic at this company. Long story short, it fucked over its employees so ruthlessly, that I'll need to write another book about that. Because you have no idea how fucked up that experience was. Anyhoot, working for this public school/charter school was equally as ruthless, insidious, and as disturbing as working in the Retail Industry.

Chapter Six
Jordan Is Not Acting Like A Supervisor

No kidding Sherlock the little voice in my head said when Ted admitted one of Jordan's shortcoming in a meeting we had on Monday, May 22, 2017. Ted was reacting to my email 'Offensive Language.' At this juncture, I wasn't expecting Ted to take my observations about Jordan's toxic behavior seriously. Again when I'd mentioned to Ted that Jordan was leaving the property, Ted said, *"You keep saying that, you better have some proof...I need dates and times."* So, what else could I say? If Ted were going to play that game, then so would I. You should've seen Ted's face when I told him how badly Jordan berated him. Ted was squirming like a fish out of water. Not to be outdone, Ted tried to change the conversation by insinuated that I could clean the entryways according to the 'Core Standards.' I'd ripped that bullshit right in front of his face. I made him sorry that he even went there. Then like a snake in the grass, Ted attacked Rachel. Again, I wasn't having any of his bullshit and defended Rachel and walked out the office with my head held high. I'd bet anything that Ted immediately called Mateo, and within a half hour, Ted was back in my face, but this time his demeanor was more apologetic. He asked me to write my, 'Concerns' about Jordan on an email and send a copy to Mateo. I did as per instructed.

A copy of my original email to Mateo and Ted and Mateo's response:

From: Lopez, Mateo
Sent: Tuesday, May 23, 2017 7:20 AM
To: King, Alexandra; Rogers, Ted
Subject: RE:

Alexandra,

Thank you for taking the time to write a statement I will get with HR and seek their recommendation. I will follow up with you as soon as I can. In the mean time we have removed Jordan form the night shift.

Thanks,
Mateo

-----Original Message-----
From: King, Alexandra
Sent: Monday, May 22, 2017 11:30 PM
To: Rogers, Ted; Lopez, Mateo
Subject:

On day one of my employment at XXXXXX XXXX and on numerous occasions after that, Jordan had told me that Ted was lazy, he doesn't want to work, nobody likes him, because he so lazy. That he [Jordan] does all the work, that Ted was demoted from XXXXXXXXX High School. That Ted was transferred to another school, but he was so lazy that they [the staff] complained and Ted was removed and sent to XXXXXX XXXXI. On more than one occasion, Jordan told me I could leave some of my work undone, so Ted would have to complete it the next day. He bragged that he often leaves some of his work undone so Ted would have to do it. Recently, while Jordan was training me to secure and lock the doors and other responsibilities for setting the alarm, he told me I could leave at 10pm, tell Ted that I'd left at 10:30pm, and that the computer wasn't working so I couldn't swipe out. During my first week at XXXXXX XXXX, Jordan told me that Blacks, Hispanics, and Native Indians go to heaven, but that White people go to hell. He simultaneously pulled out his personal cell phone and proceeded to search bible scriptures for me to read. I told him I didn't have my reading glasses, so he wanted to know if he should bring his bible to work. I told him, "No." The next day, Jordan asked me if I was ready for more bible lessons. I told him, "No," and walked away. Jordan then turned his bible conversation onto XXXXX.

Chapter Seven
Bitch Ass Jordan

When I saw Jordan after his return from vacation, I'd let him know how much of a lazy asshole he was. I told him what others before me were too afraid to tell him, i.e., that he was a sorry ass bitch.

Let me give you the background story on this scandal. Back in May, Rachel and I took our concerns about Jordan's toxic behavior to Ted and then to Mateo. But because Ted and Mateo were asswipes for Jordan, they did nothing but remove Jordan from the night supervisor position. That's why Mateo transferred Alejandro into the night supervisor position. Trust me, although Mateo told Rachel and me that the Human Resource department would 'investigate' our complaints, we also received that old misogynistic response, i.e., *It's your word again Jordan's word."* Yeah, you guessed it, Mateo threw Rachel and me under the bus. So you can imagine how embolden Jordan became. So it wasn't a surprise to me when I'd discovered a week before Jordan was scheduled to go on vacation that he wasn't cleaning the restrooms located in the

'A' corridor. When I say he wasn't cleaning, he wasn't cleaning. On Tuesday, July 18, 2017, at approximately 10:30 am, I'd walked into one of the boy's restrooms located on the first floor only to discover how deplorable it looked. I knew Jordan was responsible for cleaning those restrooms so I wasn't surprised. Summer school had commenced, and there were plenty of students occupying the classrooms in that area of the school. However, I didn't jump to conclusion, but a thought came to me later on. At 1:21 pm I took my cell phone and videotaped the boy's restroom and the adjacent girl's restroom. Then, before I'd left work that day at 6:30 pm, I took my phone and videotaped the conditions of the other boy's and girl's restrooms in the 'A' corridor. Then I'd videotaped the same four restrooms on Wednesday, July 19, 2017. That was more than enough proof that Jordan wasn't cleaning a damn thing in those restrooms. On Thursday, July 20, 2017, I took my concerns to Ted, and it triggered Ted to write this note to Jordan.

It reads:

Jordan

Be sure that you are cleaning the restrooms first thing in the morning

Thanks

Ted

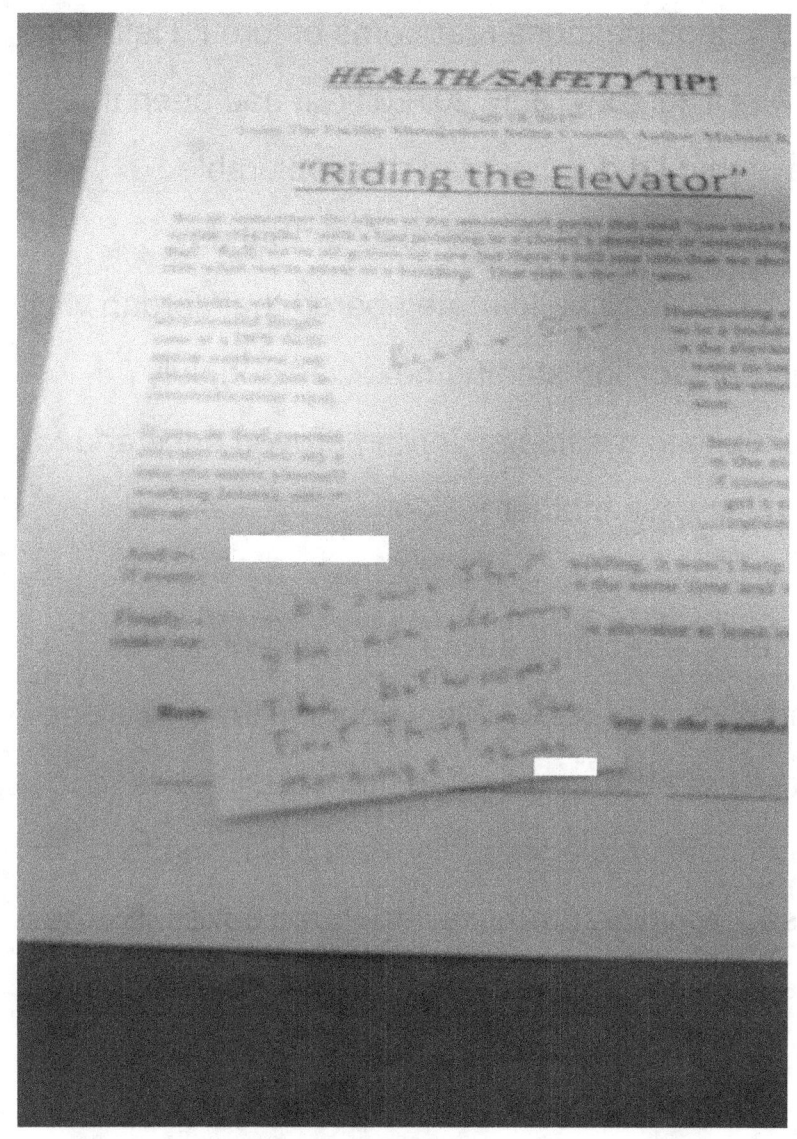

That note was left by Ted in plain sight on a table in our break room. Again, I'd videotape those restrooms before I'd left work that day. That was Thursday, July 20, 2017, it had been three consecutive days that I'd documented the deplorable conditions in those restrooms. It was also on that day, Thursday, July 20, 2017, that I'd remembered that Jordan was scheduled to go on vacation starting next week on July 24, 2017. From the sinks to the floors, Jordan proved once and for all that he was a lazy ass mother fucker.

Each day for three consecutive days I'd documented the deplorable conditions, i.e., sticky, filthy floors, filthy sinks, pee stained and smelly urinals, and stuffed menstrual boxes. I'd noticed that each day female students were still trying to discard their used feminine products into those boxes. By the third day, those boxes were overflowing. The smell was odious.

(Warning Graphic Pictures)

It didn't surprise me after I'd arrived to work at 10 am on Friday, July 21, 2017, that Ted had assigned me to clean those filthy restrooms on the 'A' corridor. I'd immediately videotaped those restrooms. The only thing that had changed, the menstrual boxes were emptied. But the lazy asshole didn't put a new paper bag inside each box.

Ted also announced that I would receive my 90 days performance review that day. Again, that bitch tried to gaslight me with his bullshit:

90 Day Review   Performance Feedback

Employee: SSN: N/A
Job Title: Custodial Helper   Date: 7/20/2017
School/Department: Date Assigned:

Instructions: Check all items relevant to the employee's position. Rate each item on a scale of one to five. Place a check mark (4) in the area provided in accordance with the following rating scale.

1 = Unsatisfactory
2 = Marginal. Below standards but making progress
3 = Satisfactory. Meets Standards
4 = Exceeds Standards
5 = Outstanding

TASK	TRAIT/ABILITY/CHARACTERISTIC	1	2	3	4	5
1. QUALITY OF WORK	Able to provide quality work free of error or waste.	☐	☐	☐	☒	☐
	Puts forth effort. Produces the desired quantity of work relative to standards.	☐	☒	☐	☐	☐
	Able to work independently without supervision.	☐	☐	☒	☐	☐
	Meets deadlines and schedules. Uses time efficiently and effectively.	☐	☒	☐	☐	☐
	Begins work at scheduled starting times.	☐	☐	☐	☐	☒
2. JOB KNOWLEDGE	Possesses the skill and knowledge to adequately fulfill the job responsibilities.	☐	☐	☒	☐	☐
	Demonstrates technical expertise and is able to apply the knowledge.	☐	☐	☒	☐	☐
3. INITIATIVE	Expends the effort and time necessary to do the job well.	☐	☐	☐	☒	☐
	Routinely shows an interest in improving his/her job knowledge and skill level.	☐	☐	☒	☐	☐
	Works well independently or within a group.	☐	☐	☒	☐	☐
	Routinely cleans, maintains, and repairs his/her equipment and work area.	☐	☐	☐	☒	☐
4. ATTENDANCE	Meets work attendance expectations. Is within the 95% attendance requirements.	☐	☐	☒	☐	☐
5. CUSTOMER SERVICE	Is dependable and responsive to customer requirements.	☐	☐	☒	☐	☐
	Maintains a good working relationship with the customers.	☐	☐	☒	☐	☐
	Is respectful to students, staff, and the community.	☐	☐	☒	☐	☐
6. SAFETY	Adheres to all safety standards in the performance of their job.	☐	☐	☒	☐	☐
	Is safety conscious and wears and maintains personal protective equipment.	☐	☐	☒	☐	☐
	Reports hazardous conditions.	☐	☐	☒	☐	☐
	Applies good housekeeping techniques in assigned work areas.	☐	☐	☒	☐	☐

	TRAIT/ABILITY/CHARACTERISTIC	1	2	3	4	5
TASK / LEADERSHIP	Trains, coaches and develops employees.	☐	☐	☐	☐	☐
	Delegates responsibility and authority.	☐	☐	☐	☐	☐
	Recognizes individual capabilities and assigns work accordingly.	☐	☐	☐	☐	☐
	Anticipates and prevents conflict within his/her work force.	☐	☐	☐	☐	☐
	Able to maintain the respect and trust of staff, peers, managers and customers	☐	☐	☐	☐	☐
	Enforces standards, displays initiative and self-confidence.	☐	☐	☐	☐	☐
	Provides guidance and feedback to employees.	☐	☐	☐	☐	☐
8. ORGANIZATION AND TIME MANAGEMENT	Adheres to priorities and deadlines. Completes work on time.	☐	☐	☒	☐	☐
	Follows through on assignments despite setbacks.	☐	☐	☒	☐	☐
	Demonstrates flexibility in responding to priorities and organizational change.	☐	☒	☐	☐	☐
	Organizes people, materials and support to get the job accomplished.	☐	☐	☐	☐	☐
	Manages multiple activities at once to accomplish the organization's goals and objectives.	☐	☐	☒	☐	☐
	Manages time, people and materials effectively and efficiently to achieve the desired results.	☐	☐	☐	☐	☐
	Arranges information and files in an efficient and effective manner.	☐	☐	☐	☐	☐
9. INTERPERSONAL SKILLS.	Demonstrates effective communication skills and is able to relate well to others.	☐	☐	☒	☐	☐
	Promotes team work and cooperation.	☐	☒	☐	☐	☐
	Supports District policies concerning Equal Opportunity, sexual harassment and diversity.	☐	☐	☒	☐	☐

Evaluator Comments: _____ comes in on time each day ready to work. She is dependable, and the quality of her work is good; meeting and often exceeds our DPS quality standard. I would like _____ to work on being more collaborative with our team at times when we are short handed and/or have extra activity in the building. She needs to be able to raise her level of productivity, to help us meet the need. _____ is a valuable member

Employee Comments: _____

Ted's comments:

Alexandra comes in on time each day ready to work. She is dependable, and the quality of her work is good, meeting and often exceeding are XXX quality standard. I would like Alexandra to work on being more collaborative with our team at times when we are shorthanded and/or have extra activity in the building. She needs to be able to raise her level of productivity, to help us meet the need. Alexandra is a valuable member of our team.

So my response was:

I Alexandra King request this form be attached to my 90 days job performance review.

It's a known fact that during the week of July 17, 2017 one of my co-workers ignored their responsibility to clean the restrooms for three consecutive days. When I say ignored, upon my first inspections on Tuesday, July 18, 2017, those hallway restrooms located on the, 'A' corridor, were filthy and the smell was odious. Yes, on the third day, I took my concerns to Jeff. So you can imagine that on the next day, Friday, July 21, 2017, I Alexandra King was given another opportunity to pick up the slack left by one of my co-workers. I can honestly say, that my co-worker left those restrooms in shambles, but because I'm the ultimate team player I'd restored those restrooms to the standard of cleanliness that you and I deserve.

My willingness to take on more responsibilities, in this case, more responsibilities left by one of my co-workers is commendable. Not only do I complete those extra responsibilities left consistently by one of my co-workers to the best of my abilities, but because I'd managed my time efficiently, I'm able to complete my own tasks.

I'm the epitome of taking on more responsibilities, managing my time efficiently, producing excellent results, and being a team player.

Anybody working for XXX, in the Facilities Department who had to clean up after a co-worker, knows what I'm talking about.

_____

Evaluator's signature   Date

That's right, I gave myself my own 90 Days Performance Review and sent it to:

> From: King, Alexandra
> Sent: Sunday, July 23, 2017 9:28 AM
> To: Human Resources, (HR Connect)
> Cc: Menendez, Lucy
> Subject: 90 Days Performance Review
>
> To whom it may concern,
>
> I have no rights to control Ted Roger's vision of my job performance. What I have a right to do is tell the entire truth.

After witnessing what I saw in those restrooms, you can bet I told that spineless bitch ass Jordan how I'd felt about his plot to intentional leave those restrooms filthy for his co-workers to clean. The next thing I knew, Jordan started singing 'Mammy,' to Ted, He said, *"Dude, what is she talking about?"* In Ted's haste to retaliate, he gave me an 'MFR.' Memo For Record. BIG mistake for Ted.

Copy of the original MFR:

TO: ▚

FROM: ▚

DATE: 08/03/17

SUBJECT: Memo for Record

Please consider this a Memo for Record surrounding our verbal conversation relating to the specifics mentioned below.

Specifics regarding a situation needing immediate improvement

I walked up on ▚ as she was verbally abusing another co-worker. ▚ had just found ▚ upon his return from his vacation and (completely unprovoked, as witnessed by ▚ the AFM) proceeded to tell him off, saying that he left his bathrooms a mess for her to clean up. This was inaccurate, the bathrooms that ▚ was asked to clean up had been used by our large summer program all day till after 3:00p. ▚ shift ends at 2:00p and so he was not asked to clean them up before he left. After I stepped in and put an end to this verbal abuse against ▚, ▚ proceeded back to the classroom that she had been cleaning and began to loudly complain and stir things up with her other co-worker that she was working with. ▚ attitude has been very negative lately, and she is having a negative effect on our custodial team.

Previous discussions and instructions with the employee, if any, on this situation and date on which employee was provided an opportunity to respond to the allegations/complaint

I have recently spoken with ▚ about similar concerns on 7/21 when I gave her a 90 day evaluation. It was communicated to ▚ at that time that she has not been a good team player, and that she needs to follow instructions from her supervisor to help out the team when we are shorthanded. ▚ needs to follow instructions and do her job without worrying what her other team mates are doing. ▚ should come to me if she has concerns with other team mates, and allow me to handle the situation.

I have received a copy of this memorandum and have discussed it with supervisory personnel. My signature below does not indicate agreement with the content of this document and I understand that I may write a memo of reply to this document.

_____   _____
Employee Name   Date

ACILITY MANAGEMENT / DEPARTMENT OF OPERATIONS •

My response to Ted's MFR

From: **King, Alexandra**
Sent: Friday, August 04, 2017 9:15 AM
To: Lopez_Mateo@ Human Resources, Connect (HR Connect); Menendez, Lucy; Rogers, Ted
Subject: Memo For Record

I understand that **Ted** is invested in protecting Jordan, but I will not allow Ted's revisionist history and inconsistency of what actually happened during the week of July 17, 2018, to be the only record on paper. On or about July 12, 2017, Kevin the Night Supervisor reported that Ted had assigned Jordan to clean the restrooms throughout the school. On Tuesday, July 18, I'd became aware that the Menstrual boxes located on the 'A' corridor were filled to capacity, and that all four restrooms were in deplorable condition. After two consecutive days, the girl's restrooms were smelly and the Menstrual boxes were overflowing. I'd took my concerns to Ted On July 20, 2017, who confirmed that Jordan was responsible for cleaning those restrooms. By the end of my shift, Thursday, July 20, 2017, Ted had left a written note to Jordan reminding Jordan to clean the restrooms.

On Friday, July 21, 2017, the next day the only improvement in all four restrooms was that the overflowing and smelly Menstrual boxes had been emptied. The deplorable conditions remained.

I'd had and will continue to take my concerns about the filthy conditions I see throughout the school to Ted. The MFR I'd received from Ted on August 3, 2019, is further proof of the favoritism being perpetrated in the XXXXXX XXXX XXXXXX School's Facilities Department.

Chapter Eight
A Video Is Worth A Million Words

A smartphone is a smartphone. I have documentation to back up my words. Shortly after Ted's MFR bullshit, I had a meeting with Mateo, Ted, and a Union Rep named Lucy Menendez. I'd made them aware that Ted saw how deplorable those restrooms look. I'd bet money, that after I'd left that meeting, Mateo asked Ted and Ted told them the ugly truth about those restrooms. Because the next day, Mateo made me an offer I couldn't refuse, i.e., transfer to another school. Mateo's tough guy disappeared, and his bitch came out.

My smartphone outsmarted Ted, Mateo, and Jordan for that matter. When I spoke, my words had conviction. When they spoke, they were grasping at straws.

Trust me; I'd loved seeing Ted and Mateo squirming in discomfort because what became apparent to them was that I wasn't lying. I'd exposed their dirty little secrets to their faces. My attitude towards the 'Good Ole Boys' club was, **'Fuck you and the horse you came riding in on.'** Ted, Mateo, and

Jordan allowed deplorable conditions to exist at that school because they only cared about their paychecks.

Trust me, Ted, Mateo, and Jordan don't want anyone to see the videos and pictures of how Jordan abandoned the restrooms during the week of July 17, 2017. Well, that's too damn bad. Oh, I know they won't hesitate, 'Playing the victim,' card. All I can say, **'Good luck with that."**

Chapter Nine
Don't I Give You Compliments

Ted honestly believed he was superior to black women to the degree that he thought his compliments meant the world to me. In reality, Ted's compliments meant nothing to me. They were as corrupt as Ted's tough guy stance. Because when it came to Jordan, Ted tough guy disappeared and his bitch came out. Ted was a sniveling coward, masquerading as a privileged white man.

On more than one occasion I had the privilege of witnessing Ted's spinelessness. On the other hand, Jordan was a complete fool. One minute he was a black-faced Al Jolson singing, 'Mammy' and the next minute he was a wanna be gangsta.

If I had to sum it all up, I'd say that the, 'Good Ole Boys' club biggest mistake was underestimating me!

Chapter Ten
The Harsh Reality

My initial approach to this chapter was a bit harsh. My belief was that this behavior, i.e., putting feces inside the urinals, smearing feces on the walls/toilets/floors, throwing full cartons of chocolate milk onto a restroom wall, or peeing all over the toilet, peeing on top of the urinals, or writing giraffe on the restroom walls, or digging inside your nose and wiping boogers on the walls, or stuffing the bathroom sinks with paper towels then turning on the water knowing that the water will overflow in the sinks and flood the floors, or stuffing the toilets with paper towels, or stuffing the menstrual boxes with trash, or trashing classrooms, or trashing the boy's/girls locker rooms, or other atrocities that made the custodian's job that much harder, was deliberate. My attitude changed when a room full of Educators told me that in some cases, that behavior was the result of abuse in the home. That put a different light on this subject. Listen up parents, some of your children are perpetrating this behavior, and some of your children are witnessing this behavior or the aftermath of this behavior. Trust me; I'm not the only one documented this behavior, and it's just a matter of time before the perpetrators are exposed. Parents, you don't want to get embarrassed knowing that your child(ren) is/are responsible for the images like the ones at the end of this chapter.

From day one of my employment, I'd saw disturbing images like these, left by what I assumed were students, but it wasn't until I'd transferred to the second school when I'd started taking pictures. These images were an everyday occurrence and were another reason why custodians quit often and abruptly.

Facilities Managers were quick to reiterate some bullshit called, 'Core Standards.' A scientific formula on time for each task custodians were assigned to do. On paper that bullshit was a fantasy, it was far from reality. The images you're about to see made the 'Core Standards' a joke. Trashed and filthy classrooms and restrooms were the new normal. In my experience and I'd suspect in many other custodian's experiences, Facilities Managers and Supervisors tried to bully us to adhering to some unreasonable times allotted to clean the classrooms, cafeteria, gym, hallways, entryways, and restroom to quality expectations.

Another problem with this, 'Core Standards' are the many incidents where viruses spreads throughout a school to the degree it was shut down. Many students and many of the teachers and administrative staff were infected and had to be sent home or seek medical intervention and then sent home. My theory to why these viruses outbreaks happen in the first place is because of the poor cleaning habits by too many custodians. I could be wrong, but from what I'd seen, I could be right. The standard of cleanliness is way below par. Any virus could easily spread in any given school like a wildfire. The saddest part, Facilities Managers, and Supervisors don't give a fuck; they're too busy protecting their paychecks. The turnover rate among custodians was and is astronomical.

WARNING: The following pictures are graphic.

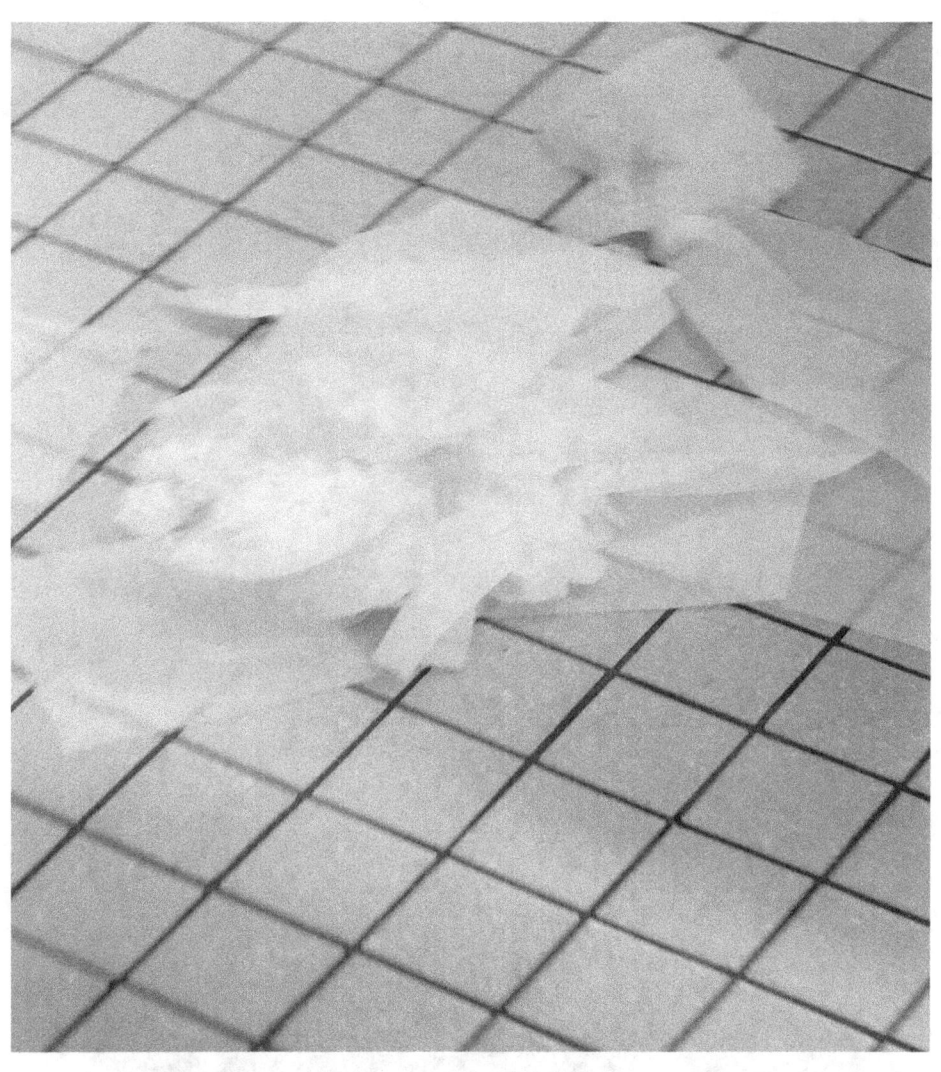

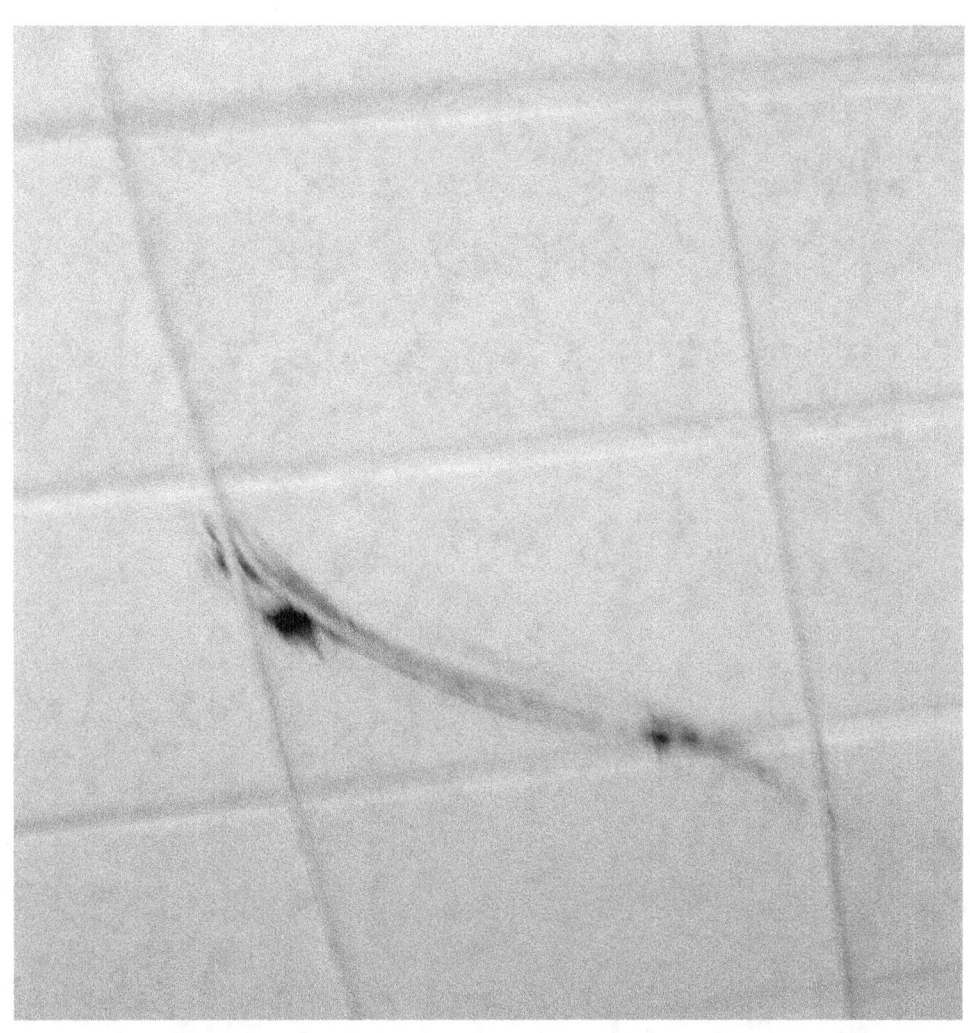

Chapter Eleven
What The Fuck

Can you imagine working with old and disgusting equipment like this? With all the money pouring into this school district, this was what I had to, and my co-workers had to work with:

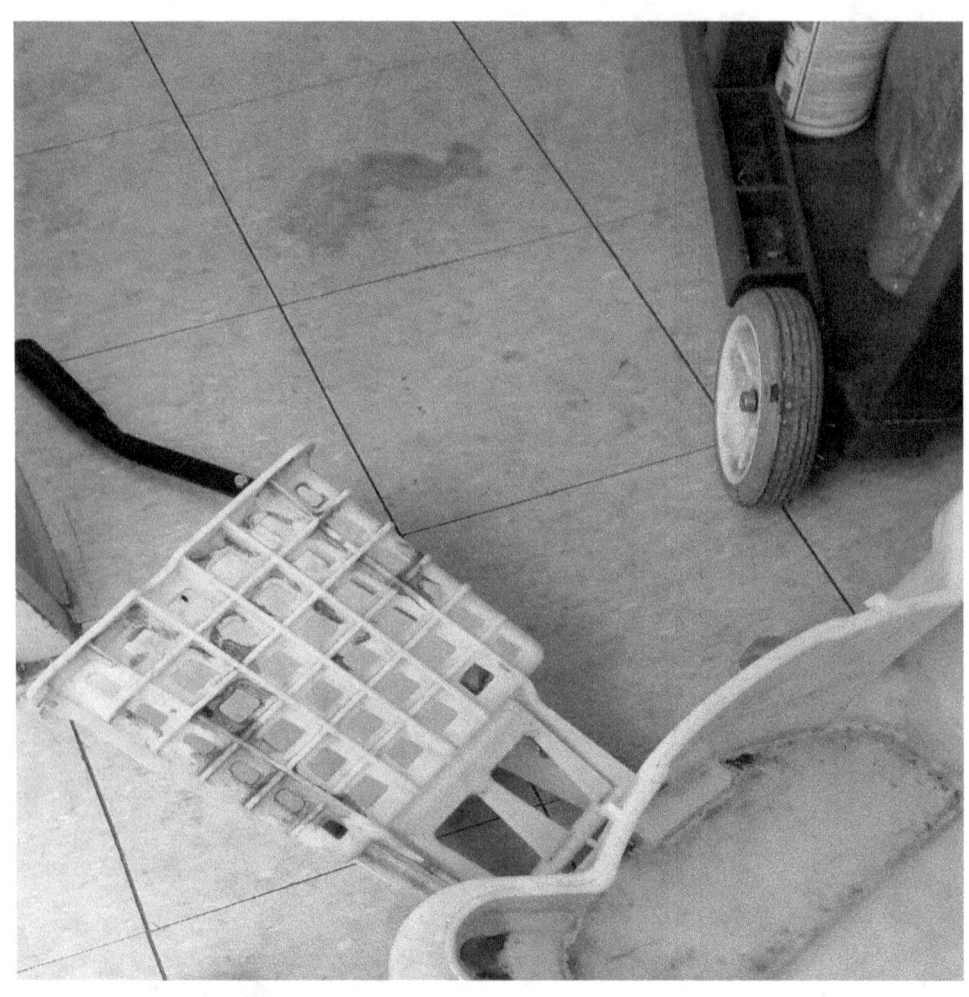

Chapter Twelve
Take Notes

Ted would never admit it, but I'll gladly tell the world that Ted is a fucking clown and that's why I'd laughed in his face in front of Alejandro. All this happened after I'd confronted Jordan and let him know how I didn't appreciate him leaving all those filthy restrooms for me to clean up. Then I'd literally turned Ted's ultimate revenge, i.e., revisionist history on his MFR form, into one of his worse nightmares. An older Black woman laughing at him, to his face. You should have seen Ted's ego go from arrogant to complete humiliation. Ted's diabolical plan was to write me up for being abusive and verbally attacking that sniveling bitch Jordan. The truth was, Jordan was Ted's cock holster. Suffice it to say, my face to face encounter with Jordan revealed just how much of a momma's boy he was.

I'd bet you that Ted won't be so quick to try and bully another Black woman. On the day Ted presented me with his, 'MFR, form, I'd entered his office dancing my ass off. At this time I was listening to songs from my cell phone and had on a pair of audio headphones. I was on cruise control. Ted was so out of his league to the degree that Alejandro probably felt sorry for him. I'd annihilated Ted in front of Alejandro. But in the back of my mind, all I could say was, *"Really Mateo; this is the best you could come up with?"* Because all Ted could say to me was, *"Why aren't you taking this seriously?* I'd told his bitch ass, *"It's Christmas in August...I'd received a gift from Mateo this morning...and now you gave me a gift."* That's the morning I'd read the email Mateo sent me concerning my recent request for a transfer. Copy of email on page 98.

Ted's GOD complex disappeared that day, and his bitch came out. He knew Jordan intentionally left those restrooms in deplorable conditions. But to intentional re-write history (MFR) with some made up bullshit proved fatal to his dumb ass.

Chapter Thirteen
Fuck You Adriana

Mateo foolishly believed that he'd backed me into a corner, when he deliberately passed me up for a transfer, then threatened me with some bullshit about working with Ted for another six months.

Copy of email I'd received from Mateo:

From: Lopez, Mateo
Sent: Wednesday, August 02, 2017 4:18 PM
To: King, Alexandra
Cc: Rogers, Ted
Subject: Transfer

Alexandra,

I noticed you applied for a transfer, unfortunately you applied a bit late as another candidate is in the process of being hired already, please don't be discourage as there is more positions available, however I did want to touch base and let you know I would need to fill your position before you got moved to the position you obtain when you do get selected on any upcoming position.

Also I wanted to reach out and let you know I have been made aware of some situations where you have been insubordinate and this can cause a big issue if discipline is followed thru with the incidents. I ask that you please just come in and take care of your assignments until you apply and receive a transfer. If discipline is issued it will hold you at your site for another 6 months. I need you to please be respectful and listen to Ted as ultimately he is your supervisor.
Thanks,

Mateo Lopez
Area Manager
Facility Management-Operations
XXX-XXX-XXXX Office
XXX-XXX-XXXX Mobile

Here's my response and the responses from HR and Mateo:

From: Garcia, Selena
Sent: Wednesday, August 16, 2017 10:23 AM
To: King, Alexandra
Subject: RE: Transfer

Alexandra
I am aware that this meeting will be scheduled and I will be a part of it. In the meantime, we expect all employees involved to treat each other with respect and professionalism. Based on the email correspondence below, I want to make you aware that this expectations does also include you.

Regards,
Selena Garcia, PHR
HR Business Partner
XXXXX Public Schools
Office:
Fax:
Students First - Integrity - Equity - Collaboration - Accountability - Fun

-----Original Message-----
From: King, Alexandra
Sent: Wednesday, August 16, 2017 10:09 AM
To:
Subject: FW: Transfer

From: Lopez, Mateo
Sent: Tuesday, August 15, 2017 10:14 AM
To: King, Alexandra
Cc: Rogers,Ted; Menendez, Lucy
Subject: RE: Transfer

Alexandra,

I will set up a meeting with you, union, Ted, and I, as this situation is now getting out of hand. I will let you know what day this will happen.

Thanks,
Mateo

-----Original Message-----
From: King, Alexandra
Sent: Tuesday, August 08, 2017 8:50 AM
To: Lopez, Mateo Subject: FW: Transfer

I need you to please tell me why I should respect favoritism in the workplace? Favoritism is negative and abusive in any work environment and Ted had on more than one occasion shown favoritism towards Jordan Thomas. The deplorable conditions Jordan Thomas left the restrooms located on the corridor, 'A" during the week of July 17, 2017, was not the first time Ted allowed deplorable conditions to exist within XXXXX XXXX School.

Alexandra King

Shortly after my response to Mateo's email threatening me about working under Ted for up to six more months, I attended a meeting with Mateo, a union rep named Lucy Menendez and Ted. I'd took Ted to the woodshed again and kick his ass to the degree that Mateo sent me this email:

> From: Lopez, Mateo
> Sent: Wednesday, August 16, 2017 4:13 PM
> To: King, Alexandra
> Cc: Menendez, Lucy
> Subject: Transfer Availabilities
>
> Alexandra,
>
> I have the following positions available:
>
> XXXXXXXXXXX- 1230p-9p, this school is off XXXXXXXXXX
>
> XXXXXXXXXX- 130p-10p, this school is off XXXXXXXXXXX.
>
> XXXX XXXX This is a morning position 530a-2p, this is located off XXXXXXXXXX.
>
> Thanks,
>
> Mateo Lopez
> Area Manager
> Facility Management-Operations
> XXX-XXX-XXXX Office
> XXX-XXX-XXXX Mobile

Mateo found out quickly that he'd messed with the wrong bitch. Not only did I transfer to another school, but as you can see I had my choice of three schools. In zero to 100 Mateo went from being the Godfather to the sniveling bitch ass coward I knew he was.

Adriana was the Facilities Manager at the school that I'd transferred to and from what I saw; she pretended to be a tough bitch. In reality, she was a pimple on Mateo's ass.

Xavier was the night supervisor and Adriana's 'Husband at work.' Xavier was cool until he got on his high horse and started ordering me around like I was his labor slave. Yeah, that impulse to treat employees like labor slaves was crazy and insidious.

Let me paint a picture of Adriana's ineptitude. That bitch was all ready to get on my ass about the filthy conditions of the 'cleaned' cafeteria restrooms she had inspected upon arriving to work one morning. That was until she found out that it was Xavier who had cleaned them. Then the bitch said, *"Oh, well that makes sense now...cause I couldn't believe you'd left those restrooms looking like that."* Proving that Xavier's standard of cleaning was way below par. However, that bitch was riding me to rush through my work like Xavier. Xavier was Adriana's labor slave, but I wasn't going to become Xavier's labor slave. I'll give Xavier credit, he tried to sabotage me, but he failed. After Adriana had inspected my work, that bitch wrote that I had 'time management' struggles. It was obvious who had stabbed me in the back. You guessed it, Xavier.

Adriana is so inept that she allowed the grounds around the school to deteriorate to the degree that some of the parents living in the area threatened to sue if the grounds were not cleaned.

Adriana's 'Mean' girl stance was straight outta the comic books. In the words of Cardi B, *"Hey little bitch, you can't fuck with me if you wanted too."*

Conclusion:
My word of advice to anyone working in an unfavorable work environment, "Don't take no shit, document. Documentation will empower you to stand up inside yourself. You are not alone.

www.ingramcontent.com/pod-product-compliance
Lightning Source LLC
Chambersburg PA
CBHW082344220526
45470CB00008B/2633